The Blueprint to Coparenting

Working Together To Do What's In The Best Interest Of Our Children

ISAIAH GARY

Copyright © Isaiah Gary, 2023

All rights reserved. No part of this book may be reproduced or used in any manner without written permission of the copyright owner except for the use of quotations in a book review.

ISBN 979-8-9879187-0-8 (Paperback)
ISBN 979-8-9879187-1-5 (E-Book)

Imprint: Independently Published

For more information about this book or the author, please visit our website: **Adversitybuildscharacter716@gmail.com**

For more information about the editor, please contact her at: saltertj@buffalostate.edu Edited by Tristin Jacy Salter, Writing Instructor at Buffalo State University

Dedications

This book is dedicated to the parents who brought forth life with someone they are not currently in a relationship with.

I pray that through reading this book you discover a new strategy, concept, or idea that assists you in effectively coparenting and working together to do what is in the best interest of your child.

I have been through the drama, arguing, and petty disputes. I am telling you; it is so much better on the other side.

There are some very practical things you can do to improve your relationship with your coparent, which can ultimately benefit your child. Teamwork makes the dream work!

And finally, to my children Egypt, Isaiah, Dawon and my bonus children Shien, Davia, and Dwayne. Always remember your Dad loves you to life. Always remember the sky is the limit and the life you dream of is within your reach. Work hard, stay focused, and always do your best.

Acknowledgements

There is no way I would have been able to write *The Blueprint to Coparenting* without God. I can say this with certainty because if it was not for my relationship with God, I would probably be dead or in jail. The transformation that took place in my life would not have been possible had I not had a relationship with him. Thank you God.

Jeanice Gary, my lovely wife, thank you for your love and support throughout this process. Also, for making our house a home and holding down the fort, so that I have time to work on my dreams and goals. You are a constant support in my life and my best friend. You listen to me talk about my dreams and goals and support everything I do. I thank God for you, and I know I am blessed to call you my wife. I love you baby.

Erica Seymour, The mother of my son Isaiah. Thank you for your willingness to put the work in to coparent effectively with me. It has been a journey to say the least. One of the things I am most proud of is the way we coparent our son and work together to do what is best for him. I pray that many of the people who read this book can make progress in their coparenting relationship and enjoy some of what we have built.

Sandra Ivey, my mother, thank you for instilling so much love in me and always telling me how handsome I was even when I did not feel handsome. Also, for telling me I look nice and building my sense of self-worth. For helping me with my children and being supportive in everything I do. I could go on and on, but I have to thank you for being a constant in my life and accepting me for me. I love that I can be my authentic self around you and let my mask down to breathe. It is a blessing to have you as a mother, and I do not take that for granted.

To all the women I know and love who I have watched struggle being single mothers, watching your strength and struggles played a role in inspiring me to write this book. I hope to inspire men to be more supportive of you and assist more with their children because God never intended for you to carry that load alone.

To all the men I know and love who have experienced challenges with coparenting, you also inspired me to create this work. While it is written to you, I hope some of the women who read the book can gain an insight into what we go through as men and learn new strategies and ideas for how to engage with us. Some of you work hard to coparent and are met with unwarranted resistance. Others have an opportunity to coparent at a higher level and be more involved in your children's lives. Some may fall in the middle. No matter where you fall, I want you to know I love you and I am here for you. I want to see your relationship improve with your coparent and your children. I believe in you, and I hope this book inspires you. Shout out to all the Dads who are taking care of business and actively involved in their children's lives. We don't hear it enough. I'm proud of you.

Black Diamond Circle, my men's group. I thank you for holding me accountable as a man, for pushing me and listening to me as well as for being my safe place to let my mask down and providing me honest feedback. Being a part of this work has taken me to another level and I am forever grateful.

To all my friends and family who have supported me throughout this process. I thank you. Trey, Mia, Jose, Gary, Mukendi, my book coach Kara Oliver-Perez and everyone who has encouraged or inspired me throughout this process I say, thank you.

Contents

Dedications .... *iii*

Acknowledgements .... *v*

Introduction 1

Chapter 1 – For Your Information (FYI) 7

Chapter 2 – My Why 13

Chapter 3 – Support Is More Than Money! 19

Chapter 4 – This Too Shall Pass 29

Chapter 5 – Supporting on a Different Level and Becoming The Best Version of Yourself 43

Chapter 6 – You Can't Double Back!!! 65

Chapter 7 – Humbling Yourself 71

Chapter 8 – Healthy Boundaries 77

Chapter 9 – Postpartum Depression 85

Chapter 10 – Gift Giving 89

Chapter 11 – Forgiveness 93

Conclusion 103

Introduction

What does parenting mean to me? Parenting means loving your children unconditionally, even when it is hard. It is protecting, providing for, and teaching your child(ren). There are times when you will do things you do not want to and make sacrifices so that your child can have a better upbringing than you did or an upbringing as good as yours was. Positive parenting also means being patient with your children and making time for them regardless of what is going on, along with providing guidance and words of encouragement. It is complementing your children and helping them build their self-esteem while also correcting them when they are wrong, providing discipline when needed, and giving tough love at times. Overall, parenting is preparing your children for the world as they are a reflection of us, we owe it to them and to ourselves to raise them right.

The reason we as men need to coparent effectively has nothing to do with the mother of our children and everything to do with our child. Once your relationship with her is over, one could make the argument that you have no obligation to her because she is no longer your woman. She may even be with another man. This in itself makes coparenting challenging.

Investing in this relationship is taking ownership on another level. Again, you are not doing it for your child's mother, you are investing in this relationship for your child.

You have to get past the circumstances under which your child came into the world. It really does not matter. Whether it was a one-night stand, an affair, a friend with benefits who got pregnant, or you planned to have children is irrelevant. Even if she finessed you into having a child, it does not matter. If you need to establish paternity, do that. Take a paternity test. Once paternity is established, there are no excuses. You do not get to say I didn't sign up for this or she got a new man or whatever bogus excuse you try to tell yourself that justifies not being involved in your child's life. You have to ask yourself is this the man I want to be? Is this the type of father I would want? Even those questions leave room for error because you can tell yourself, "at least I'm doing better than my dad did for me" and that's lame. The real question is, am I being the parent my child needs? There are many benefits to coparenting, which I will discuss, but if you take nothing else away from this book remember this. You show up and be the dad your child needs. You also coparent effectively for your child. Perspective is everything. If you look at coparenting as something you are doing for your child's mother, that makes it harder to do. If you look at it from the lens of, I am coparenting effectively because it is what is best for my child and I love my child, it makes it easier. Keep the right perspective, especially on the challenging days. Believe me there will be challenging days. Keep your head up and stay strong. You got this!

What is coparenting? Coparenting is defined as sharing the duties of raising (a child) (used especially of parents who are separated or not in a relationship). That is one way of looking at it and I agree that in simplest terms that definition is correct. I however have my own definition. The zayfinition is working together with your coparent to do what is best for your child and ensuring your child has the best quality of life possible. Yes, I made up my own definition and this is the place I operate from. How we frame things is extremely important. I like the zayfinition not only because I made it up, but because I feel it more accurately defines what coparenting should look like, it is also a call to action. The zayfinition requires more accountability and encourages teamwork. My definition has an outcome attached to it, an end goal, which helps us stay focused on why we need to coparent effectively. Coparenting effectively is work, it is challenging but rewarding and requires you to humble yourself in order to develop a relationship you can be proud of. It requires you to put petty differences aside in order to work together to do what's in the best interest of your child. Coparenting at the next level requires teamwork, communication, empathy, maturity, emotional intelligence, growth, personal development and so much more. The question we must ask ourselves is are our children worth it? If I told you learning to coparent more effectively would help your child and give them a better quality of life, would you make that investment? Do you believe that your child would benefit from seeing their parents be able to be cordial and work together to meet their needs? These are questions you have to answer for yourself. I asked myself these questions and my answer was emphatically, yes!

Investing in my relationship with my coparent was one of the best decisions I have ever made, and my son is all the better for it because of the relationship I have with his mother. I could simply pay child support and fall back, picking him up only on my scheduled days, choosing not to have anything to do with his mother. However, what would this accomplish? The question truly becomes, would that behavior benefit my son? Are any of those situations going to help my son become the best version of himself? The answer is no, none of these options would help build his character. Some people may say yes that whatever they're doing is the best possible situation based on their circumstances. They may be correct. For me the answer is no. None of those options would be best for my son. None of those options would help him become the best version of himself. Even though my relationship with his mother failed, my son is my responsibility, and it is my responsibility to make sure he has the best quality of life possible. Your coparent is not your enemy, and you don't have to have beef. That is an outdated way of thinking, and some of us need to get over that.

Why I wrote this book: I wrote this book because many children do not get the opportunity to have both parents present and actively engaged in their lives. Even when they do, they are often subject to arguing, bickering, petty behavior, custody battles, and ineffective coparenting. I believe that improved relationships between coparents will lead to children who feel loved by both parents and they will reap the benefits of having both parents involved in their lives. I have personally been able to improve my relationship with my son's mother, mediate an agreement regarding visitation, (which is legally in place, but we do not necessarily use anymore) have my child support reduced and then stopped, and more importantly we get along and discuss our son regularly. I'm proud that we have been able to develop a friendship through everything we have been through. It was not easy. I will say it again: it was not easy! It took a lot of effort on both ends, and we still have disagreements or get into it from time to time. However, we both have our sons' best interests in mind, and we work together to make sure his needs are met. That's the bottom line. Everyone will not reach that place and I am not saying reading this book is going to get you there. It is my hope that by reading this book, you will have some takeaways that will assist you in developing, strengthening, and maintaining your relationship with your coparent in order to work together to make decisions and take actions that are in the best interest of your child. I am a masculine man, and this book is written from that perspective. I understand that there are all different types of relationships and variances in the role of a Father. This is written from a masculine male's perspective. It would be too complex to include all the other variants. This is about my experience, from my point of view and that is all I am qualified to speak on. I would hope anyone who reads this is able to develop new tools for their toolbox to help them coparent more effectively.

CHAPTER 1

For Your Information (FYI)

The challenges of coparenting- Being a parent is not an easy job. In fact, it is the hardest job I have ever had. Add in your coparent and it can get really interesting. To start there is the personal aspect of the failed relationship. That is complicated in itself, then there's the child. The child is being raised in two separate households by two unique people with different ways of doing things. Which parents' way of doing things is the right way? That's a trick question. So now you are raising a child with someone who potentially has a different mindset, approach, and set of values.

Ideally you get on the same page and work together. You do what's in the best interest of the child and put petty differences behind you. If only it was that easy right? The reality is you will have disagreements, you will want to prove your point, you will get angry because things didn't go your way, you may feel some type of way about your coparent and the way they do things. Another challenge of coparenting is being the bigger person and forgiving when you feel wronged. Although this is a challenge, it is necessary.

Why coparenting is so important- Coparenting is important because children benefit from having two functional parents in their lives. Children need to know that they are loved, and the absence of either parent takes a toll on the child. We've gotten a long way away from the traditional family and I get that. Somewhere along the way we normalized "single parents" and being baby mommas and baby daddies. All relationships don't work out, life happens. People have children and grow apart. Sometimes people were never in a "relationship" to begin with. Again, life happens. Divorce happens, relationships fail, and sometimes it is better for parents to coparent than to stay together. All that being said, I believe a child needs both parents. There are things a child gets from a mother that they do not always get from a father and vice versa. It is in the child's best interest for the parents to be able to work together to raise the child. Everyone's situation is different and there is no cookie cutter way of approaching coparenting. Assuming both parents are functional and have a healthy relationship with the child, coparenting is important. Some parents are toxic, abusive, or unhealthy for the children to be around. Those types of relationships are outside of the scope of this book. I am not a clinician, and I would recommend that someone who is unhealthy for their children to be around seek professional help. Coparenting can be a wonderful experience when the two parents put the work in and put petty differences aside to do what is best for their child. It is important for a child to see their parents getting along, working together, and being on the same page. It benefits parents to be on the same page because it's not as easy for the child to play games and manipulate the parents. When it comes to correcting or disciplining our children, it is important that we stand as a united front. When we do not stand as a united front, it sends mixed signals and can create room for our children to manipulate us. It's a game changer when we stand as a united front, set boundaries, enforce boundaries, and hold our children accountable in love. Holding children accountable can be challenging for some parents, which makes it even more important that we learn to work together as a team. When the world corrects or disciplines our children, it will not always be in love. A child knowing that both parents love them is the ideal situation. It's even better when they can see the parents be cordial, respectful of each other, and work together to meet the needs of the whole child.

Chapter 1: Key Points, Guiding Questions & Challenges

Key Points:

1. Coparenting is difficult. The child is being raised in two separate households by two unique people with different ways of doing things.
2. Ideally you do what is in the best interest of the child and put petty differences behind you.
3. Children benefit from having two functional parents in their lives.
4. Sometimes it is better for parents to coparent than to stay together.
5. It is generally in the child's best interest for the parents to be able to work together to raise the child.
6. Some parents are toxic, abusive, or unhealthy for the children to be around. Those types of relationships are outside of the scope of this book, and I recommend that those parents seek professional help.
7. It is a gamechanger when a child sees their parents getting along, working together, and being on the same page.

Guiding Questions:

1. What commitments do I need to make in regard to this chapter?
2. Do I coparent on a high level?
3. What opportunities for growth do I have as a coparent?

Challenge:

I challenge you to keep an open mind while reading this book. By keeping an open mind, you create the space to rethink everything you believe to be true about how you must interact with your coparent. Your situation may not be ideal and that simply means you have an opportunity to improve your relationship. Maybe your relationship with your coparent is cool, but it could be better. Either way, when we change the way we see things, the things we see will change. I challenge you to keep an open mind. Will you accept this challenge?

CHAPTER 2

My Why

I can remember being her buddy in Lamaze class. I forget the exact wording, but the instructor said something to the effect that I was her partner, and we were in this together. I must admit I had some resistance to being a father at first. The pregnancy was not planned, and I was not ready to be a dad.

I had already raised a child only to find out I was not the father, and that hurt me deeply. I questioned the legitimacy of my next child, but DNA proved that I was in fact the father. I was already parenting because deep down I knew he was mine. I needed confirmation though. Once I got it, it was a weight lifted off of my shoulders and I was pumped up! This was redemption! My own little man who was born a day after me, my Junior, my baby. Words alone cannot explain the joy I felt. My dad died when I was nine and my step dad at fifteen. I did not know the first thing about being a dad, but I knew I had to figure it out.

The short amount of time I had with my dad on those weekend visits did not prepare me for fatherhood. I knew my dad loved me and I do have a handful of memories with him. Like him tapping me on the shoulder and stealing food off my plate when I turned around or walking to church with him. My dad could sang! My dad used to record the church service and I would sit with him and watch him tape the service. One of my fondest memories is my dad taking me to see Mortal Kombat when it came out. Although I did not have a long time with my dad, I have a handful of memories I will never forget and I know my dad loved me. Yeah, my dad loved me.

I did learn some things from my stepfather, but he had his struggles as a man and eventually passed away also. Prior to him passing away, I remember him leaving us and being with another woman and family. We did have some good times though. He taught me about defending myself, how to rib on people, how to put my pants on a hanger, and took me fishing. I remember him sleeping in church with sunglasses on. He was hilarious and had a great personality. One thing that stands out about him was that he aint take no stuff. I have some good memories with both of them. May they rest in paradise. Be that as it may, I did not want my son to grow up without a dad like I did because I know how that made me feel. I wanted my dad, and he could not be there for me. There was no way I would allow that to be my son's experience. I did have some men in my life like my God father who I saw on visits to his house. He took time to teach me things a young man should know how to do like cutting the grass, scraping, and took us to do fun things too. I know he cares about me and loves me.

Over time his relationship with my Godmother did not work out and I saw less of him as well. All in all, I was blessed with a few good men in my life, but most of the men in my life taught me how to survive in the streets as opposed to how to be a father, or a productive member of society. I learned a lot about how I did not want to be watching them. I'm thankful that they taught me how to survive because those skills were necessary and a part of who I am today. Growing up I resented my uncles and male relatives for not being more involved in my life. As a young man, I can remember feeling like one of my uncles should have came to save me from situations I was in during the rough times. He lived in the suburbs and had a beautiful life from what I could tell.

One day I decided I would not be a victim anymore and that I had to let that animosity go. A recent conversation shed light on the situation with my uncle and offered a different perspective on what I have been feeling. The mature thing to do would be to sit down with my uncle as a man and talk to him. But then again for what? On some level I want closure, but he is not losing sleep over not being there for me when I needed him. I say all this to say if I can learn to be a father with little to no example or guidance, you can too. There is work to be done and our kids are worth it. They deserve the best version of us being actively involved in their lives. In my opinion, there is no acceptable reason not to be involved in your child's life. Children do not ask to be born. We decide through our actions to bring forth life. How the child ends up here is irrelevant. Children are innocent. As they grow and get older, they may do things that we do not approve of, and some relationships can become toxic. As kids though, it is our job to raise them, teach them, and mold them. We should do everything in our power to be involved in our children's lives and to raise them. Excuses mean nothing.

Chapter 2: Key Points, Guiding Questions & Challenges

Key Points From This Chapter:

1. As coparents we are in this together.
2. Circumstances are irrelevant and you do not have to be ready. When you have a child, you take responsibility.
3. Growing up without a father sucks. Do not allow that to become your child's experience. Excuses mean nothing to me or your children. They need us.
4. If I can learn to be a father with little to no example or guidance you can too.
5. Our children deserve the best version of us actively involved in their lives.
6. There is no acceptable reason not to be involved in your child's life.
7. We should do everything in our power to be involved in our children's lives and to raise them.

Guiding Questions:

1. What commitments do I need to make in regard to this Chapter?
2. Do I understand that my presence as a father is needed and how important having a relationship with my child is?
3. What opportunities for growth do I have in this area?

Challenge:

I challenge you to have a conversation with your coparent about how you can best work together to meet the needs of your child. (If you're legally permitted to)

During this conversation, listen more than you talk. This will help you get a better understanding of what she wants and needs from you as a coparent. Do not become defensive or swell up with pride, even if she becomes emotional. The purpose of this conversation is to identify ways you can help her and take steps to improve the relationship. Take notes. From your notes develop an action plan to address making improvements as a coparent. It may look something like this:

What she said: "I'm stressed and I'm tired" or "I need a break!"

Action item: Spend time with my child on Saturday and pay my niece to watch her overnight. Now she has time to herself on Saturday to do what she wants to do.

This is an example, but from your notes start identifying solutions and ways you can help out more. She will appreciate it, even if she is not in the place to say she does. Before you start taking action, ask if she would like you to help. She could just be venting to you because she is frustrated.

CHAPTER 3

Support Is More Than Money!

Although many men make the mistake of thinking I am not with her, so that is not my problem. I offer a different perspective on this. Now there is some truth to that statement. If you are not in a relationship with the mother of your child, then she is not your priority. Your home should be your priority and that should be made clear.

However, this does not mean you can't support her. There are several ways a woman needs to be supported and it goes way beyond money. Money is one way she needs to be supported. Whether you pay child support or have a private agreement, it is unrealistic to believe a woman can take care of your child without your financial help. While some women can, they shouldn't have to. We made the child together and we need to take ownership and provide for our children. Every situation is unique, and I cannot tell you exactly what your arrangement should look like. What I can tell you is that she needs your help, and you should assist her financially. I put myself on child support to start out once our relationship failed. Eventually she wanted more money, and I told her *"take me to court"!* And she did.

They did not care about what I had done or want to see all my receipts I had stuffed in a footlocker bag; they took 17% of what I made and asked if I was okay with that arrangement. I said, "Can I make a counteroffer?" I countered her at twenty five dollars more than what she had originally asked for. I couldn't believe it. I would have made out better giving her what she had originally asked. Over the years we both grew, and she reached a point where she did not want child support anymore. We made a private agreement and negotiated terms for me to come off of child support. So, while there is no formal order in place, I still support my son and his mother financially. I send her money, buy clothes, and give her money for things she wants to do. I also do for my son when he is with me.

I want to point out that the time I have invested in our relationship makes this possible. You may not get one without the other. Meaning, your child's mother may be more willing to work with you if you have a positive relationship with her. I mean, even if she can take care of your child without you, do you really want her to? What does that say about you as a man? If I wrote her off and did not support her in more ways than one this agreement may not have been possible. I offer more than money, and the support I offer is worth more than money. That is a major key. I will discuss some of the other forms of support I offer which I believe helped build and sustained our relationship.

Other Ways To Show Support:

Childcare-She needs a break. She needs time to herself without the child or children. Everyone needs time to themselves, don't you? Selfishly in the beginning, I did not want my son around other men. So I would keep my son on weekends or have him at my mom's to give her time to herself. One day I was visiting my godbrother and talking to him about it and he said, "She got needs too Bro". That was so simple, yet profound. Just like we have needs, our child's mother has needs too. I have to take a moment and shout out my mother. My mom is a major support in both of our lives and helps out tremendously with my son. She has helped us with him since he was born and seldom if ever says no. I understand this is a blessing and may not be your situation. Some of our parents are deceased, some live out of town, some are not fit to keep the kids, I get it. If there is a trusted family member that can help with your child(ern) and take a load off of her back, it is worth exploring. You may need to pay them; however, this is a small price to pay to give your child's mother a well needed break. This is a life hack. She will appreciate the time to herself and that you are taking ownership of childcare.

That's all fine and well, however we have to do our part also. If our kids are always with our family members and never with us this will be a problem also. As with almost everything in life, balance is important. Whether it is one day a week, a few hours, the weekend, an overnight etc. We have to make time for our kids. In my opinion, time spent with the children is more important than money. Not for your child's mother, but for the kids. Make time to be a dad and make memories. I digressed.

My son's mother and I had an agreement mediated early on. The agreement literally breaks down what days my son stays where, who he stays with during breaks from school, and what holidays he spends at whose house. It also lists who he is with on odd years and even years. This is extreme in my opinion, but we needed this level of intervention early on because we could not agree on things as mature adults. I know something is wrong with both of us every time I share this story with people by the look they give me. The bottom line is that fathers need to help with childcare. If the child resides with the father, then the mother should assist with childcare. If we need to pay, we need to do that, we also need to make time to spend time with our children. One thing I do is keep all my children on Friday night. It has become a tradition. We watch movies, play games, and I order pizza. That is our time. Sometimes I'm so tired I fall asleep, but Friday is our day, and they know that. At the same time, my son's mother knows she can do whatever she wants on Fridays. I also keep my son on Wednesdays. We have a weekend agreement; however, Friday is our day. You have to come up with an agreement that works for you. It may require you sacrificing a day/ night that you used to do something else. I can assure you the investment is worth it! My schedule is structured the way it is because a few years ago I had two jobs. A full time 9-5 and a second job once I got off, that I worked (Mon, Tue, Thurs, and Sat.) I just stuck to my childcare schedule. I have more flexibility now and I see my son on days outside of my schedule. It is good for both of us.

Doing your part- Although you are busy, she is busy too. Since she is busy that means we must stretch ourselves and do more. Depending on how you were raised, your mother may have been superwoman! She provided, cooked, cleaned, disciplined, and nurtured us. I mean momma did it all and, in many situations, we may not have had a man in the equation. When you grow up seeing that, it can become normal to you. If you are not careful you can look at your child's mother as weak because your mother was so strong. My momma was super woman! Whole time, she should have never been in a position to have to be. Your father or her man should have been right by her side helping her. Too often women are put in situations to have to do everything and that was never how it was supposed to be. For some of us, our mother was not actively involved in our lives, she didn't take care of us or do the things we thought a mother should have done. I understand that, and I empathize with you if that was your reality. Depending on the severity of the dysfunction you grew up in, it may be beneficial to speak to a therapist to work through what you have experienced. I attend biweekly counseling and it is one of the best decisions I have ever made.

Regardless of your upbringing, and the role you saw your mother play, your child's mother should not have to take care of your child alone. She did not bring forth life alone and she should not have to care for your child alone.

Transportation- We should assist with transportation because children have busy schedules. They have to get to and from school, to childcare, to grandma's house, to birthday parties, Doctors Appointments, extra-curricular activities, Sheesh! You catch my drift?

Realistically speaking we cannot assist with all the transport for our children. What we can do however, is prioritize assisting with transportation. We can make changes to our schedule to accommodate our children's needs and take pressure off of their mother. We can pick them up from school, take them on Doctors' appointments, take them to school functions, pick them up for visits and drop them off. This is not anything outside of the ordinary. It also gives us time to talk to our children and spend time with them. We do not want our child to be the last one picked up from places or even worse stranded somewhere. Remember, when we take stress off of the mother of our child we lighten her load and can potentially take stress off of our children. When your child's mother is in a good place, feeling good, and less stressed, you set the stage for her to show up for your children as the best version of herself. Regardless of how you may feel about her, you need her to show up as the best version of herself for your child.

Listening- She wants to and needs to be heard. It is easy to write off what someone else is saying. Sometimes my son's mother calls me and I have no interest in what she is saying. Other times I am too busy to listen to what she wants to tell me, and sometimes I straight up don't care what she has to say. All that being said, I learned to listen to what she was saying and what is not being said. Hearing what is not being said can get deep and become confusing. So let's focus on what she is saying. I learned to actively listen to what she is saying to me. It is not easy, believe me. However, it is worth it. We can listen to what someone is saying and not hear them. This is why actively listening is key. Actively listening involves not talking and genuinely listening to what others have to say. It is paraphrasing or being able to summarize what they are saying. It is using the paralanguage, e.g: *"Um, um hmm", "I see, wow."* It is blocking out distractions and listening to what she is saying. In person it is maintaining eye contact, nodding your head when appropriate and giving your undivided attention. I have learned to listen to understand and not to respond. This is a major key. When we listen to understand we get more out of what is being said. Even when I don't want to listen, I listen. When I'm too busy to listen, I tell her that. I say something like:

> *"This sounds important, I am too busy to listen to what you are saying right now, can we please talk about this later when I can give you my undivided attention?"*

More times than not she respects it. If it is something that is really important, we simply have to make the time. When we listen to what she has to say and she feels heard, we get better results. We cannot be dismissive of her thoughts and feelings even when we know we are right. We must become better listeners.

Chapter 3: Key Points, Guiding Questions & Challenges

Key Points From This chapter

1. There are several ways a woman needs to be supported and it goes beyond financial support.
2. Although some women can provide for our children alone, they should not have to. We created these children together and we need to take ownership.
3. Offering more than money in terms of support goes a long way towards strengthening the coparenting relationship. (There are always exceptions to the rule)
4. Your coparent needs a break sometimes. Schedule time to spend time with your children. If you are really busy, have a trusted family member help out so that your coparent can have a break.
5. If you are not careful you can look at your child's mother as weak if your mother was strong.
6. We should be assisting with transportation to and from places.
7. Listen to understand and not to respond.

Guiding Questions

1. What commitments do I need to make in regard to this chapter?
2. Do I support my coparent to the extent that she needs to be supported?

3. What opportunities for growth do I have in this area?

Challenge:

I challenge you to be more supportive of your coparent. You may be paying child support and spending time with your children, but is there more you can do to support? You may be extremely supportive, and if you are that is phenomenal. However, if there is room to be more supportive and do more to take a load off of your coparents shoulders which could potentially improve your child's quality of life, why wouldn't you? Will you accept this challenge?

CHAPTER 4

This Too Shall Pass

The rough days- There will be rough days. There is no way around it. Sometimes I get it wrong, sometimes she gets it wrong, sometimes we both get it wrong. We have these heated disagreements that bring out the worst in each other. I say things to hurt her and she says things to hurt me. When this happens, we both lose. We lose because our focus is not on being the best parents our son can have. Our focus is on winning the battle, proving our point, or being right. I feel terrible after I flip out on her. One, because I have reached a place as a man in which I am disappointed with myself when I let my anger get the best of me. Secondly, because it can become a situation in which the retaliation is "oh you can just get your son on your days". Third because when I am angry with someone, I need time and space. During that time and space, I am not the coparent she needs. More times than not this blow up is over a disagreement in parenting style or a lack of communication. We are both passionate people. On the surface, we are both trying to prove our point or explain why we are right. Then someone throws a low blow or says something disrespectful, and it becomes personal. Now the gloves are off, and it becomes a heavyweight boxing match. We exchange shots until one of us submits, is really hurt, or hangs up the phone. Looking back at this process from afar, I should never be in a boxing match with a woman. Whether the boxing match is verbal or physical it's really a no-win situation. Even if I win, I lose. We have to learn to control our emotions with our coparent.

During the rough days, time and space usually does the trick. I may need to go three days without talking to her or maybe even a week. I am still present for my son during that time. Sometimes I just need a break, and I am sure she would say the same. Eventually the ice gets broken. Something will come up that we need to talk about, or I will usually crack a joke, or send her a thoughtful text message explaining why I feel how I feel or said what I said before it became personal. Before you know it, we're back talking again, and back to coparenting on a high level. The work that I put into the relationship and my consistency as a father helps during the rough times. She knows that I always have my son's best interest at heart. I think it also helps that I don't miss a beat or treat my son any differently when we are going through a rough patch. Relationships are work and we both have to keep working to make this thing work. Some days are easier than others, but we never give up! We fight to coparent effectively because we both want what is best for our son. Even though we have different opinions on what that may be at times.

Arguments- There will be times when we strongly disagree. It is almost inevitable. What's important is how these disagreements are handled and what we do after the argument. Depending on the household you grew up in or how you were raised, seeing people argue may be normal to you. That may be the only way you saw people handle their disagreements. I dare to say that was wrong. There will be times when emotions run high and there are arguments. However, we need to become better communicators and learn to express ourselves without arguing. I come from a family of people who are passionate and can become extremely emotional. I am aware of this and have learned to hold my tongue over time and to take the emotion off of what I need to say. It does not always work. Sometimes I become extremely emotional and act a plum fool. I'm human. We should never argue in front of our children. They do not need to be exposed to that. Children should not listen to adult arguments and be exposed to vulgar language and potentially see how ugly things can get. That is not for their ears. Do your best not to argue in front of your children. Go into another room, have the children leave the area, do your best not to normalize arguments and expose them to arguments. Coparents are going to disagree. Having heated arguments in front of children does not give them a positive example of how to manage conflict and children mirror behavior. We have to learn to effectively manage conflict with our coparent. As the man in the situation my focus has become not becoming overly emotional. When I become overly emotional with my son's mother I lose. It's really a no-win situation. She is emotional by nature. I am learning to stick to the facts and remain calm. When I feel I am being disrespected and start becoming overly emotional, I tell her, "I'm not willing to talk to you when you speak to me that way, let's talk about this later when we both cool down." If I am really upset, I say, "I'm just going to talk to you later because this is about to go left" I can feel it rising up when I'm about to say something crazy or disrespect her. In my opinion, it is better to revisit the conversation because conversation is irreversible and once I say something it's out there. I can apologize, but once I say something crazy it's too late. Now I have to hear about what I said five years later. We all want to be heard and, in many instances, we believe we are right. We're arguing our point and it can be frustrating when the other person does not hear us or agree with us. My son's mother and I had some very ugly arguments early on. I have incorporated these strategies to avoid those because when we are arguing, mad at each other, and not communicating, the person who suffers most is my son. Arguing has cost me time with him, stress with her, stress and anxiety in general. I stick to my guns about what I am feeling, but I take the emotion off of what I am saying and work through what I need to say. I have also learned to put myself in her shoes and think about how she might be seeing or feeling about a situation. There is value in that.

Transactional Analysis (TA) is a psychoanalytic theory and method of therapy, developed by Eric Berne during the 1950s. Transactions refer to the communication exchanges between people. During a conversation with someone, the person starting the communication will give the transaction stimulus and then the person receiving this stimulus (or message of communication) will give the transaction response. Transactional analysis is the method used to analyze this process of transactions in communication with others.

It requires us to be aware of how we feel, think and behave during interactions with others. Transactional analysis recognized that the human personality is made up of three "ego states"; each of which is an entire system of thought, feeling, and behavior from which we interact with each other. The Parent, Adult and Child ego states and the interaction between them form the foundation of transactional analysis theory.

Transactional analysis says that effective communication can only take place in adult mode. When we are in parent mode we make "you statements". Such as, you need to, you should, you better etc. When we are in child mode we make "I statements". For instance, I hate when you, I have to, I don't want to etc. Lastly when we are in adult mode, we are making "we statements". Examples of this are, we should, we could benefit from, we will etc. I have put transactional analysis in my tool belt, and I use it regularly. I even redirect conversations when I see my son's mother is in child mode to bring the conversation back to adult mode. I still get it wrong when it comes to arguing, it is a learning process as with anything else. The difference is now I feel bad when I lose it. I think to myself how could I have communicated better? How could I have said what I needed to say without it becoming an argument. I do not want my son to see or hear me disrespect his mother and my mouth can get very disrespectful. I do not want to hurt her. When she is hurt my son sees it. When she is angry, she's not the best version of herself and may not be able to give my son the best version of herself which is what he deserves. My mother says sometimes you have to "eat crow". I take that to mean sometimes you have to take peoples stuff in order to maintain the relationship. The key word is sometimes. Do not allow counterproductive communication to become the norm. You have to teach people how to treat you. After arguments I find myself apologizing. Especially if I said something inappropriate. It doesn't change what I did, but I think it helps. Once cooler heads prevail, I explain my position or express my feelings calmly. I reassure her that my intention was not to hurt her. I also understand that I do not get a pass because my intentions were not to hurt her. My intentions are irrelevant, what matters most is the end result. If I hurt her or disrespected her then that is what happened. My challenge is to become a better communicator and be more self-aware, so that I can avoid arguments and diffuse situations before they become problematic.

[1] Heather Murray, "Transactional Analysis Theory & Therapy: Eric Berne

Transactional Analysis Theory & Therapy: Eric Berne", Last modified February 14, 2023, Transactional Analysis Theory & Therapy: Eric Berne (simplypsychology.org)

You catch more flies with honey- I don't know where my mother got this from, but it is a saying that's stuck in my head. What it means is that you get more of what you want when you are nice (sweet) to people. I have applied this in my life, and I encourage you to do the same. Sometimes we have to kill people with kindness. Conversely, sometimes we have to teach people how to treat us, but we are not going to get into that right now. Kill them with kindness. It does not benefit us to be hostile, rude, standoffish, unapproachable, mean etc. When we are nice many times we get better results. Not always, Sometimes I am nice and I still get called a jerk. There are no guarantees. However, this works. I can be sweet to my son's mother without being sweet on her. Doing things like making her laugh to keep things lite. On holidays I take my son out to buy her a present. If he cannot go, I buy a gift myself and have him give it to her. I am generally just nice to her overall. Even when it's hard. I get better results from her this way. I also have to set the tone for how my son treats women, particularly his mother. I need him to see me be patient with her, be kind to her, help her, show her that I care about her and respect her. I believe this will go a long way towards him showing her those same things. As men we have to set the tone. Be sweet even when you feel sour. Show her the patience that she may or may not have received from another man. Treat her with dignity and respect even though she may not display those values. You catch more flies with honey. Do your best not to be mean, be sweet. Even though ain't nothing sweet. After you have been sweet and patient and she is still behaving inappropriately, you might have to show her ain't nothing sweet. Remember, there are times when you have to teach people how to treat you. You do not have to match energy, tell her about herself or "put her in her place". Just tell her I am not willing to speak with you when you behave this way. When you are ready to talk I will be prepared to listen and complete this conversation.

Let it go- you can be mad, but don't stay mad. I believe that the way someone treats you is a reflection of how they feel about their self. So when I get into it with my son's mother sometimes I step back and think what is she going through? What is she feeling? Is she overwhelmed? Worried? And other times I'm like oh she's just being a jerk and I got time today. So yes, we get into it and sometimes I shut down. For me, this serves as a defense mechanism. Sometimes I shut down when I'm angry to stop myself from making inappropriate statements or being disrespectful and to take time to reflect. I have weaponized my silence before also and I try not to do that. Like I have intentionally not spoken to my son's mother to punish her and I have to find more productive ways of handling being angry. Not to mention, she may have needed a break from me also. Maybe the whole punishing her with silence thing is something I made up in my mind and she could care less. Whether it is or is not a thing, I have to be better than that and continue to work on learning to communicate more effectively.

The reality is, I made lifetime decisions with this woman and I am going to deal with her for the rest of my life. So I can become angry, but I have to get past the anger. My son's mother and I need to be able to communicate about my son. We need to work together to meet his needs. When we are angry and not speaking to each other that is counterproductive. It does not serve anyone. I have learned to humble myself and get over being angry. I could stay mad, but that is a waste of energy, and it is not in the best interest of my son.

There will be times when your child's mother does and says things you do not like or agree with. There may be times when she says or does disrespectful things, and you will likely become angry when she says or does it. There will likely be times when she makes you angry. It is ok to be upset. We have feelings too and we do not have to minimize our feelings. I had to learn this for myself. What I'm saying is take some time to get over it and let it go. Every situation is unique, and there are situations in which someone violates you on another level. In that instance it may be necessary to set healthy boundaries. You may need to give that situation time and space. You may have to show that person that their behavior is unacceptable and you are not willing to communicate with them when they behave that way. Set the boundary, enforce the boundary, hold the person accountable. In some circumstances that may be necessary. Whatever you do, whatever happens, do not allow it to impact your relationship with your child. Assuming you can still see and spend time with your child, do it. Do not allow the ignorance of your child's mother or your own ignorance to become a reason that you do not spend time with your child. Your responsibility is to your child and that is the only person's opinion you should ultimately be concerned with. Coparenting on a high level is amazing and I want it for everyone. Make sure your child knows you love them. The day will come when you have to answer to your child about being present or absent in their lives.

Build a bridge and meet in the middle- We as parents have to get over this mentality that our way is the only way and that we have to win. Many times, if we take a step back and think, there is a win win. A situation where we can both win. The question is how do we get there? I'm glad you asked. We build a bridge and meet in the middle. So, assuming you stand on one end of an issue and your child's mother stands on the other end, you would meet in the middle on said issue. By doing this you both get some of what you wanted out of the situation. For example, my son's mother wanted to take my son South to see her family and we are supposed to share holidays. I did not resist her even though holidays are important to my family, and I did not want him to go. I let him go and spent more time with him than I normally do on another holiday. It is good for my son to travel, have life experiences, and spend time with the other side of his family. By being stubborn and having to have things my way, I would have stopped him from having this experience. Not to mention, there will be times in which I need my coparent to be flexible with me. One hand wash the other, both wash the face. We have to learn to compromise when it comes to our children. Ultimately our actions and decisions should be those that are in the child's best interest. It should not be about us winning, making our point, or having our way. That is childish. When we learn to work together and give up being right for what's right for our children, good things start to happen. We have to put the child first.

Chapter 4: Key Points, Guiding Questions & Challenges

Key Points for this chapter:

1. We should not be going tit for tat with our coparent.
2. We may need time and space from our coparent. This time and space should not change how we show up for our children. After we take our time and space the goal should be getting back to coparenting effectively. Time and space should not be a long-drawn-out thing. Holding grudges is counterproductive.
3. Arguments will likely occur. We need to become better communicators and learn to express ourselves without arguing.
4. If you do argue, do not argue in front of the children.
5. It is ok to revisit a conversation if you are extremely angry or overly emotional.
6. Become a better communicator and be more self-aware, so that we can avoid arguments and diffuse situations before they become problematic.
7. It is okay to be upset or angry, but do not stay angry.
8. Learn to look for the win win situation.
9. You do not have to always win or have your way. This is not Burger King.
10. Compromise with your child's mother, do not compromise your terms as a man.
11. You can get more of what you want from people when you are nice to them.

12. Sometimes we have to teach people how to treat us.

Guiding Questions

1. What commitments do I need to make in regard to this Chapter?
2. Do I handle conflict with my coparent effectively?
3. What opportunities for growth do I have in this area?

Challenge:

I challenge you to commit to working through the hard times with your coparent. Fight or flight is real. Unfortunately, too many people choose flight and in doing so damage their relationship with their child. That could be because they see it as a package deal and decide if I'm not with this woman, I am not going to help raise my child. Or whatever reason people come up with for not parenting their children. I do not want to try to get in people's heads. What I do know is it happens. I can see how some men could want to throw their hands up and walk away. Some women put you through so much that you just do not have the fight in you to deal with it. I am not okay with men walking away from their children. At the same time, they should not have to go through hell to see their children and be involved in their lives. People should not use children as a weapon or use them to hurt their coparent. That is foolishness. All that being said, we are better together as coparents. We may not want to believe that, but it is true. Children benefit from having both parents in their lives and seeing them be cordial with each other at minimum. There will be hard days and sometimes coparenting will be stressful. We can however work through our differences and work together to do what is best for our child. Will you accept this challenge?

CHAPTER 5

Supporting on a Different Level and Becoming The Best Version of Yourself

Guidance- There will be times when the mother of your child needs guidance. This can get sticky. Depending on the relationship she may or may not be open to your guidance. It is not wise to assert your opinion on her. That can blow up in your face. Here is an example of what I mean. I'm efficient with money. I really want my son's mother to be more efficient and make better decisions with her money. I pushed and pushed until one day it became an argument. I was wrong for asserting my opinion when she did not ask me for it. If she wants to buy a thousand gum balls with her money, that is her business. I only need to give her my opinion when she asks for it. We have developed a relationship and friendship to a point where she asks me for advice from a man's perspective, on career moves, and on various situations. I am able to give her guidance on various situations because of how I have positioned myself as a man. I'm consistent, stable, and I practice what I preach. She listens when I speak and values my opinion. I don't necessarily remember her saying that to me, however she keeps asking which tells me she appreciates it. When I have time, I give her guidance on various situations. Depending on the severity of the situation, I make time to talk. Sometimes I ask her for advice or her opinion on a situation too. Luckily my son's mother is very intelligent. I respect and value her opinion as well.

The mother of your children has to feel safe enough to ask you for guidance and respect you enough to receive it. I am not saying my son's mother listens. She hears me, but sometimes she does not listen. Another important point about guiding your child's mother or any other woman for that matter is actually guiding them somewhere. The blind cannot lead the blind and you cannot expect a woman to follow your guidance if you don't know where you're going or give solid advice.

It is important that we become the best version of ourselves. Not to guide the mother of our children, but for ourselves and for our children. When we are the best version of ourselves and taking steps towards becoming the best version of ourselves, we are in a different place mentally. Some of you may be asking how do I become the best version of myself? I would say that is a personal journey. Defining success and/or becoming the best version of yourself is personal. I can however share some things I have done on my journey to becoming the man I always wanted to be. Which I am still on by the way. Every day is another day to learn, grow, and make progress. How do you eat a large elephant? A small chunk at a time. Anyhow, here are some things I do or have done.

1. **Reading-** My mom always said "if you wanna hide something from someone put it in a book". Abraham Lincoln once said, "my best friend is a person who will give me a book I have not read". Both of these quotes resonate deeply with me. When you are hungry you eat. If you do not eat or go long enough without eating, you will die of starvation. Feeding your brain is equally important and that is what reading offers. It feeds your brain. Sometimes you are so busy you do not have time to read a book. Luckily, they have these things called audiobooks. Buy one and rock out. I typically read business and self-help books. I really learn a lot and I have something to pull from when having conversations or providing people with guidance. Being well read is a strength. I strongly encourage you to read. Read to your children also. Whoever said reading is fundamental was not lying. A lot of strategies I implement in my daily life and wisdom I have come from reading. There are secrets to success in books. I'm telling you reading changed my life.

2. **Listening to motivational speeches or sermons-** By feeding my brain, I make progress towards closing the gap between the man I am and the man I want to be. I find encouragement, motivation and words of wisdom to help me face the daily challenges life throws at me. I strive to start my day with something positive and control the tone of my day. If we do not eat, we will die. Our brain is no different, we have to feed our brains in order to grow strong and survive. I find comfort in knowing I am not alone and that other men have gone through things I am going through or have experienced. We can learn lessons through other people's lived

experiences. I also find jewels to help cope or deal with different situations that arise. A good speech or sermon will have you charged up and ready to get busy! Start your day with something positive and feed your brain. You have to find what works for you. My go to speakers are Eric Thomas, Les Brown, TD Jakes, and Jim Rohn. Sometimes I listen to Tony Robbins and Dr. Myles Monroe. You can listen to my content on my YouTube channel *Adversity Builds Character*. Check me out and get you some of this ghetto gospel. Again, you have to find what works for you. You may prefer one style over another, but find someone you enjoy listening to and tap in.

3. Starting counseling- I recently started counseling. It took me time to gather the courage to go. I did not want someone all in my business and in my head. Growing up I buried a lot and never dealt with it. When you are in survival mode you just have to keep pushing. There was not time for counseling and all that. I did not see the value in it. My thought process was that "I'm good, I'm making it through, I'm surviving". I have overcome all sorts of adversity and hardships, so why would I need to talk about it? The thought of enrolling in therapy has crossed my mind before because I have worked in schools with youth and had other jobs in human services, but I never acted on it. One of my boys started therapy and we would talk about it. He said something I will never forget. He said "okay you good, but why walk around with weights on your feet and unresolved issues holding you back". I'm paraphrasing, but that was what he said. Another man I know spoke to me about counseling and his experience also. When I heard other men talk about their experience and how it was a benefit and not a burden, I started to feel more comfortable with the idea of counseling. It got to a point where I made a commitment with my brothers to speak with a few counselors and then schedule an initial intake session. I did it. My first counselor was cool, but I didn't really feel a connection to her, and I didn't feel like she understood me. Once I convinced myself that she wasn't a good fit for me and stopped attending my sessions, I was back to square one. However, I had the benefit of attending a few sessions and understood the value in seeing a counselor. I recently started with a new counselor, and I feel good about it. She is more like a sister or cousin that I can talk to. I can talk to her about anything, and I do. It feels good to have someone help you reframe things and see things from a different perspective. It also helps to have someone who is unbiased tell you when you are misreading a situation or looking at it the wrong way. We are starting to address trauma from my childhood, relationships, trust issues, and more. It feels good to have someone I can tell how I really feel without a fear of hurting her feelings or making her angry. I say all that to say, if you feel you would benefit from having a counselor, give it a shot. Enrolling in counseling was one of the best decisions I have ever made. Counseling is something I never wanted but needed more than I could have ever imagined. This may be a good platform for you to work through things you need to work through which could lead to more meaningful and fulfilling relationships. I am doing the work I need to do to heal from the trauma and pain and suffering I have experienced throughout my life. Therapy is a process, and I am so happy that I have chosen to begin this journey.

4. Joining a Men's group- If you had asked me three years ago if I could see myself joining a men's group and sharing my thoughts and feelings, I would probably have laughed at you. I did not have the best relationships with men for a number of reasons. I had my boys I was close with and a few friends I trusted, but I have never really been the type to open up to men I don't know. That's just not how I operate. Hell, I don't tell the men I know and love everything. One day a friend of mine told me about a men's group that would be meeting and having discussions and he said I would be a good fit for it. I checked it out to see what it was about. At first, I was like what is this? Men were holding me accountable for things I did and did not do, we were being vulnerable with each other, and having deep conversations. It was different, I had never been a part of something like this. The men I grew up around did not talk like this. Fast forward two years later and joining my men's group is one of the best decisions I have ever made. We hold each other accountable, encourage each other, push each other, celebrate each other, and embrace each other. It is truly a brotherhood and being in my men's group has helped me in closing the gap between the man I am and the man I want to be. Having a support group of men to bounce things off of and talk things through with is a beautiful thing. Having a brotherhood of men who tell me when I'm wrong and challenge me to be better is a Godsend. There may or may not be a men's group available for you to join. If there is not a men's group available to you, you can create one or develop the types of relationships I'm describing with men you know and trust. Trust is a key component. If you have a circle of men you can call on, depend on and trust, a circle of men who hold you accountable and call you out when you are wrong you are blessed. As you deal with the complexities of coparenting, having a circle of like-minded men will be an asset to you.

5. Furthering my education- I love learning and still strive to learn something every day. Sometimes I learn from something I watch on tv, other times I learn from something one of my kids tell me, sometimes it's something a student tells me, and sometimes I learn a lesson from something I see happen. School is not the only way to learn. I learned a lot about how to move by watching other people's mistakes. If you pay attention, you can learn a lot.

I did however learn a lot in school, and I do take education seriously. I learned how to open up my mind, how to work well with others, public speaking, human interaction, and was exposed to a diverse group of people. By going to school, I added value to myself and separated myself from my competition. My education has afforded me the opportunity to step into certain positions. I made more money per hour and was able to work smarter not harder. When I worked jobs I hated it motivated me to go to school and to become more so that I could do more. I remember a former manager telling me how he would be district manager of the organization if he had furthered his education. The person who was the district manager was not as qualified as he was, but he had his four-year degree, and he did not. I can remember thinking to myself I never want to be in that position. When I was in a car accident my chiropractor told me to go to school because I would no longer be able to do physically demanding labor. I listened to him.

The bottom line is you get paid based on how valuable you are. So add value to yourself. You don't feel like college is for you? Learn a trade, learn how to operate a business, or sell Real Estate. I do not know what your interests are but add value to yourself. You do not want to work a job you hate. You also want to be in position to take care of yourself and help with your children. If you have to work three jobs to provide and take care of yourself, then when do you have time for your children? Become a lifelong learner, further your education, and add value to yourself. My children attended my graduations and saw me cross the stage. Graduating and going to college is normal for my family now. Malcom X once said, "education is the passport to the future, for tomorrow belongs to those who prepare for it today." Truer words have never been spoken.

6. Being grounded spiritually- Every man is his own man and I believe every man should do whatever he needs to do to be spiritually grounded. That may be meditation or a religion, I do not know what that looks like for you, but whatever it is, make sure you are spiritually grounded. For me praying and listening to gospel music helps on the rough days. When I have to dig deep I can listen to a word to get me back on track. My faith sustains me. I won't get preachy on you, just know that when things get rough, you will need to have faith that things will get better. You will need something to pull from to keep pushing forward. I am a Christian who respects other people's religions and freedom of religion. Over the years I have developed knowledge of different religions and take things from different religions. I know this is extremely controversial and some will not understand it. My position is that your walk with God or the universe is personal, and you need to do what you need to do to be okay. During Ramadan, I fast in solidarity with my Muslim brothers and sisters. Occasionally, I listen to Farrakhan and I respect the unity Muslims have. I make it my business to learn more about their practices and beliefs. There are very practical lessons one can take away from that. Although I am not a Jehovah witness, I agree with their position on holidays. Some people drag holidays out. We won't get too far into that though. I pay attention to how Jewish people move as well. A friend of mine in high school was a Wiccan. I say all this to say do what works for you. Although I am a Christian, I still take the time to learn about other people's religions and apply what I learn where I see fit. Being spiritually grounded is extremely important.

7. Challenging myself and stepping outside of my comfort zone- Complacency kills and we have to get comfortable being uncomfortable. Some men choose to play it safe. They do what is comfortable and do not stretch themselves. That is one way to live. I say live life with no regrets. Motivational speaker Les Brown says, "live full and die empty". That's what I'm talking about. Blessings take place outside the comfort zone. We have to stretch ourselves in order to have the life we really want. It is hard, but it's worth it. We cannot keep doing the same thing expecting different results. I have learned to make it a priority to do things that make me uncomfortable or things I have never done before. That is the spice of life. I would rather take calculated risks that could change my life than to play it safe and be stuck. It is very easy to tell yourself lies and believe them. No excuses! Push yourself, challenge yourself, and get outside of your comfort zone. Thank me later.

8. Being mindful of who I spend my time and energy on- This should have been number one because it is so important. There are people that charge us up and make us feel good about ourselves and then there are people that drain us. Some people add value to our lives and the relationships are mutually beneficial, others only take, and the relationship is one sided. Everyone does not deserve your energy. We have to be careful not to let people emotionally drain us. You need all your energy to work on your work and to be the best father you can be. There are times when we have to ignore people and not give them a reaction, sometimes we have to walk away from people, and sometimes we have to let people win. It doesn't make you soft, you are protecting your energy. Every battle is not yours to fight. You have a child who is depending on you. If you are emotionally drained, you are not giving your child the best version of yourself.

Time is our most valuable asset. You can lose money and get it back, however, when you waste time, you can never get it back. Take a moment and write down all the places you waste time. Valuable time that could be being spent with your children or working towards your goals. I am not judging you as I waste time too, however I am aware of it and consciously working on being more efficient with my time.

Okay what did you come up with? Where are you wasting time? Are you playing video games too much? Spending too much time on social media or watching tv? Talking to your friends about foolishness? Only you know what wasting time looks like for you. The bottom line is stop wasting your precious time. You cannot get it back. When you are in a better place mentally, you are better equipped to deal with the challenges coparenting will throw at you. Sometimes you cannot waste your emotional energy on your child's mother. It is ok to set boundaries and say "I'm not willing to talk to you when you behave this way" and then talk to her after cooler heads prevail. You are not required to allow someone to disrespect you because you have a child with them. Protect your peace at all costs.

9. **Developing a solution-oriented mindset-** We can talk about problems all day or play the blame game and argue over who's right and who's wrong. We can prove our point and talk about everything that is wrong. Coparents can attack each other and point out each other's flaws. It does not change the problem. The problem is still there and still needs to be addressed. When we develop a solution-oriented mindset we are operating on a higher level. Don't just tell me the problem, give me a solution and tell me how we can fix it. Having a solution-oriented mindset does not change the fact that problems will arise. It helps you see problems from a different perspective. You start to see the alternatives. You can develop solutions and then go back and handle the problem with a different mindset. It might look something like this. I understand you're upset; you have every right to be. I can see how this might make you angry. I was thinking about it, and I have a suggestion if you are open to it. What if we did XYZ? It would take care of the dun

dun dun then you would have more time on the whatchamacallit and everyone wins. What do you think of that?

Did you see what I did? I validated her feelings instead of dismissing them as trivial. I empathized with her. Then I offered a solution, so she made the choice for me to help solve the problem. After that I offered the solution and asked what she thought of it.

This is important because while she is upset because she is overwhelmed or anxious, I have already formulated a solution. I can just say it in the moment, however, how I set up offering the solution is also important. I model self-control and calmness which hopefully helps her calm down. I give her the solution when she is ready for it and she feels better, in an ideal situation. The point is when you can offer solutions to problems you are seen in a different light, and you can avoid unnecessary drama. Or at least look the drama in the face with a sense of self control and neutralize it and restore order. You have to have a strong context to do this, and you cannot become emotional with her if she becomes emotional. Always be thinking of solutions. It will not serve you to only focus on the problems.

10. Developing my emotional intelligence- Emotional Intelligence is the capacity to be aware of, control, and express one's emotions, and to handle interpersonal relationships judiciously and empathetically. I remember learning about this concept in graduate school and it blew my mind. I think of it as being aware of what the other person is feeling, being aware of how I am feeling and handling the situation accordingly. Learning self-control changed my life. When I was younger, I was angry, and I made bad decisions while I was angry. By the grace of God, I did not destroy myself. Emotional intelligence and self-control are skills you can learn too.

11. Checking my ego- This one is extremely important, and it took me a long time to get to where I am today. I say it that way because I am still a work in progress. I still have my days where my ego gets the best of me. Pride is bound in the heart of a fool. Do not let your ego get the best of you. Being full of foolish pride can cost you time with your child, lead to you being on bad terms with your coparent or being in unnecessary drama. There is a time and place for everything. There are times when you need to stand on what you say. As a man, there are times when you have to have non-negotiables. At the same time, every battle is not yours to fight. At times you have to swallow your pride and let things go. Sometimes you have to walk away. Whatever you do, do not let your ego get the best of you. Check your ego.

I did all of these things for myself. Not because of my child's mother or anyone else. That being said, all of these things contribute to my ability to maintain and develop my relationship with my coparent. The mindset and place I'm in is very important. She sees me as a resource and not a liability. Again, if we were on bad terms and she did not, I would still be working to become the best version of myself. The bottom line is when you are in a good place mentally and operating on a high level you are better equipped to guide your child's mother and any other woman. You will also be more fulfilled and feel better about your life. My list may not be yours and that is perfectly fine. These are examples of things I do in pursuit of happiness. Remember that movie?

In order to become the man we want to be we have to do the work. It is very uncomfortable at first, but blessings happen outside of the comfort zone. We have to grow as men in order to be the father our children need and the coparent the mother of our children needs. Small disciplines practiced daily goes a long way. I don't want to get too deep, but if we die daily to what we know or feel is right, we can learn new habits and new ways of thinking. When we replace old habits with new habits and develop new ways of thinking and being we allow ourselves the opportunity to live a better, more fulfilled life. When we grow and change, it creates room for us to improve relationships and take them to the next level. When we improve relationships, and they evolve we set the stage for more meaningful interactions, and we see things change. Relationships are extremely important. I learned to produce results through relationships. The relationships you have matter more than you can imagine. The relationship with your friends, family, business associates, and colleagues are all important. When it comes to coparenting your relationship with your coparent is of the highest importance. If we can get this thing right and develop new norms around coparenting, I believe we will see a change in our children. I believe we will see less daddy issues, abandonment issues, and issues our children experience as a result of not having both parents actively involved in their lives. When we change the way we see things, the things we see will change.

Supporting her dreams and goals- You may or may not always like the way the mother of your child behaves. She may not carry herself in a way that you approve of or would like for her to. I feel you. However, when she is doing right or trying to put herself in a better position, we should support her. This can look a lot of different ways depending on the relationship. It could simply mean keeping the kids so she can study for a test, go to school or do her homework. It could mean listening to her vent about her day. It could mean giving her encouraging words. I understand that every man has a different situation, so this can look very different. The bottom line is that if she is doing something to better herself, we should be supportive. Your coparent becoming a better version of herself translates to her becoming a better mother for your child. It is good for your child to see their mother set and accomplish goals. Her being in a good space mentally is good for your child. Your child's mother being able to do more for herself and your child is good. Her dreams and goals are within her reach and if you have the ability to help her reach them it may be a worthwhile investment of your time. Assuming there are not any serious issues or legal issues. My family and I supported my son's mother while she made her way through school, and it was totally worth it. She worked and went to school, and it was a lot. She went to school for her Bachelor's and then went back for her Master's. Then she turned around and got licensed. I am extremely proud of her and all that she has accomplished. I am not intimidated by her success, hating on her or anything like that, and that is how it should be. Selfishly I love that my son was able to witness that process. He saw us both go through school and finish school. Being educated is now a norm for us. We expect greatness from him, and he knows that. I am one of my sons' mothers biggest cheerleaders, I support her dreams, I encourage her, I speak life into her, I advise her, I am in her corner, and she does not have to question that. If the mother of your child is doing something to better herself, help her. Even if it is just keeping the children longer or another day so that she can do what she needs to do. It is good for our children to see their mothers win.

Sacrifice- Sometimes you have to do things you don't want to do. Not always, but sometimes we have to make time for things that may not be convenient, take us out of our way, or things we do not see as our job. Reason being it takes pressure off of our coparent and gives them a much-needed break, allows them to rest, or to finish something they need time to finish. In my opinion we should just volunteer to do things. For example, when my son's mother is telling me all the things she has to do, at times I say I'll do that or I got that. I understand that she carries a big load. My son splits time between us, but primarily resides with her. So that means she has to deal with a lot. Honestly speaking she is responsible for more than I am. I fill in the gaps. I used to say I'm too busy because I'm working two jobs, I'm going to school, etc. Now I feel like that's not a good enough excuse. Even though most times it's true. I am a busy man. I still have to make time to do things I don't want to or feel like I have to do. Here is an example of what I mean, she drops my son off at school and I pick him up. One morning she calls and says I have an important meeting to prepare for, can you take him to school. Now I would be well within my rights to say no, because that is not the agreement and I do what I'm supposed to on my end. However, if I have the time and means to help her, 9 out of 10 times I make the sacrifice and go. Why? The first reason is because she needs help, and it is my job to help her. The second reason is because I understand relationships on a different level. Relationships should be mutually beneficial. Meaning they should benefit both parties. Let me make it plain. When I do things for her, sacrifice, or help her, it strengthens our relationship. Strengthening our relationship benefits me and my son. I am not helping her with that in the forefront of my mind, it's an added benefit for doing something she needed me to do. Not to mention it results in a bonus interaction with my son that I otherwise would not have had.

Be patient with her- This is a hard one. I struggle with this and sometimes I get it wrong. When a woman has a smart mouth, says ignorant things, insults you, challenges you, disrespects you, says things to emasculate you, hurts your feelings, or your pride, it can put you in a very uncomfortable situation. When we are angry and our emotions get the best of us, we lose. Even when we feel like we won in the moment. It is easy to lose your cool and say something crazy back to her. We get into a verbal battle, and we say things to hurt each other. I have found myself in verbal wars where we would go back and forth and say the most hurtful things we could think of. It would get really intense. Whether in person, on the phone, or even via text messages. We would bump heads about something, and the gloves came off. We brought up the old and the new. We traded blows like heavyweight champions. I can remember setting up my kill shot and going for the knockout blow. See when you know someone intimately you know what hurts them and once the gloves come off it becomes ammunition. Truthfully, I wanted to hurt her and make her cry. I would say the most disrespectful things I could think of. Over time, as I matured, I would feel bad after these exchanges. They were normal to me because I grew up arguing with my sister like this. Eventually I started to outgrow this behavior and reached the point where I would regret what I said as soon as we got off the phone, or I sent the text. Over time I reached the point where I no longer wanted to hurt her. It was counterproductive and worked against me. Early on it cost me time with my son. Looking back on it, I would be so angry and use so much emotional energy that I was not focused on my goals and the things I needed to do. This counterproductive way of communication needed to stop. It took time, it did not happen overnight, and sometimes we still get it wrong. Each one of us has had to be the bigger person and stop ourselves. Many times, it was me stopping myself. I have reached the place now where I say "I'ma call you later because this is about to go left" or "I'm not willing to talk to you when you behave this way, I'll call you back". Maybe that is not the best way to handle the situation, but it keeps me from saying something crazy.

Another time I demonstrate my patience is when she makes a mistake or forgets something. I could go crazy, get angry, call her names, or tell her to figure it out. Sometimes I do have to tell her "figure it out" or help her think through a situation because I am not available to help. We already discussed helping her. I'm speaking to how we react to her making a mistake or forgetting something. Remain calm and do not become emotional. This takes a level of emotional maturity. Your instincts may say tell her how stupid that was or ask her what the hell was she thinking. Do not do it. Do not become overly emotional or kick her while she's down. Remember we have a solution-oriented mindset. We are not enablers but the least we can do is not overreact and then offer solutions to the challenge if she is open to it. After all, we want grace when we make mistakes don't we?

She is wired differently than you are. She has a different decision-making process than you do. She is not you and you cannot expect her to do what you would do. Be patient with her. It goes a long way. She may not say it, but she will appreciate you being patient with her.

Chapter 5: Key Points, Guiding Questions & Challenges

Key Points from this chapter:

1. There will be times when the mother of your child needs guidance, only provide guidance when she asks for it. Otherwise, it could blow up in your face. You can speak your mind, but do not be surprised if she snaps at you.
2. The mother of your children has to feel safe enough to ask you for guidance and respect you enough to receive it.
3. You cannot expect a woman to follow your guidance if you do not know where you are going or give solid advice.
4. Becoming the best version of yourself is a journey. I have shared 11 things I've done to develop myself and become a better man. Anything I have done to better myself you can do. Take the first step, whatever that may be for you and begin working to become the best version of yourself.
5. You become the best version of yourself for you. Not for your child's mother. By becoming the best version of yourself, you position yourself to be in a better mindset to develop and maintain a relationship with your coparent. You interact with the world differently and the world interacts with you differently, when you put the work in.
6. We can produce results through relationships. We have to learn to build, develop, and nurture relationships.
7. If the mother of your child is doing something to better herself, support her. By bettering herself she ultimately becomes a better mother for your child.

8. Sometimes we have to do things we don't want to do in order to help the mother of our children.
9. Be patient with your coparent. Extend the same grace you would want to receive.

Guiding Questions:

1. What are three things I can do to work towards becoming the man I always wanted to be?
2. What are some things I can do to be more supportive of my coparent?
3. What opportunities for growth do I have in this area?

Challenge:

I challenge you to support your coparent on a different level. To rethink everything you know to be true about how you interact with her and support her. Hit the reset button. Think of supporting her as an investment. By helping her and investing in your relationship you could potentially see a big payout in your coparenting relationship. You could reap a great harvest from your child seeing you support your coparent that strengthens your relationship with your child. I cannot guarantee it, but it worked for me. It is worth a shot. What would you lose by being more supportive? Will you accept this challenge?

CHAPTER 6

You Can't Double Back!!!

Either you're in or you're out! Stop hitting that if you don't wanna be with her. This can be a tough one because there is usually a level of comfort here. Possibly even convenience when it comes to meeting your sexual needs and hers. If you have no intentions on being with her, stop having sex with her. You are sending mixed signals and she may see it as more than what it is. Truthfully you might as well. There is a difference between the emotion of love and the emotion of sex. Unfortunately, lines get blurred, and people confuse the two. It is never a good idea to double back.

If it's over, be coparents and work together. Give each other space and room to date other people. Being intimate blurs the lines. This is challenging, I'm acknowledging that it is, but it is necessary. Sometimes it takes time to get over each other and to accept that the relationship did not work out. You may not want to accept that you are better off coparenting. However, when you know the relationship will not work and you do not want to be together anymore, intimacy should stop. People fail to realize that sex is more than a physical act. It is mental too. So you can tell yourself

I'm good, we're just taking care of each other's needs, but how often is that the plan and someone catches feelings? Being intimate with someone brings up all types of feelings. Feelings that are counterproductive when you choose to coparent with someone. What do I mean? I will give you an example.

Jim and Tammy decide they do not want to be together. They decide that it is best for them to coparent and strictly focus on their children. They have history and they both have sexual needs. Jim decided to move on and is dating Vivica. He likes Vivica but there is just something about Tammy. One day he goes to pick the kids up only to find out they are over at their grandparents. Tammy looks wonderful today and Jim is extremely attracted to her. He makes his move and Tammy consents to his advances. They both enjoy themselves and Jim goes on about his business. Three days later Jim sees Tammy out at dinner with another man while he is out with Vivica. He tries to play it cool but becomes emotional. "Where are the kids?" Jim yells. Tammy responds they are with my mother and proceeds to introduce the two men. Jim is in his feelings. He goes off and says, "I ain't tryna meet this sucka" and calls Tammy a dirty name. His ego is hurt, and he cannot reel himself back in. He blurts out, "I bet she ain't tell you I glazed them donuts the other day, did she?" The gentlemen says huh? Jim says I frosted that toaster strudel fool. The other day! You sitting up here at dinner with my left overs. Now Vivica is irate and walks off, Jim has ruined a perfectly good relationship with Vivica over ego and his inability to control his sexual desires. Tammy is humiliated and the man tells her "lose my number bag lady, you done missed yo bus". Tammy is angry with Jim for becoming emotional because they agreed before becoming intimate that there were no strings attached and it would stay between them. Now they are bumping heads and arguing, exposing each other on social media, it is a complete mess. Good story right? Although fictional in nature things like this happen every day. While fictional in nature, the story demonstrates how messy coparenting can become when coparents continue to be intimate after the relationship is over.

Jealous boyfriends bust out car windows, physical altercations occur, coparents become pregnant, people stop talking and allowing each other to see the children. Small situations become big situations because feelings are involved. You catch my drift? Being intimate with your coparent with no intentions of being together is a dangerous game to play and it complicates things. If you don't want to be with her don't hit it. I know it might be convenient. I know you have history and you might want to prove you can still hit that even though she has a new man. It does not serve you! If you don't want to be with her don't hit it! If you don't want to be with her don't hit it! Save yourself the drama and headaches that come with being intimate with a coparent you are not going to be with. There can be a weaning process. It can be difficult, but it is worth it. Find someone else to be intimate with and focus on raising the children together. It keeps drama down when you stop having sex with your coparent. Believe me when I tell you, stop it!

Chapter 6: Key Points, Guiding Questions & Challenges

Key points from this chapter:

1. Stop having sex with your coparent if you have no intentions on being with her.
2. If you are sleeping with her and do not intend to be with her, you are sending mixed signals and being intimate blurs the lines.
3. Sex is more than physical. It is mental too.
4. Being intimate with someone brings up all types of feelings. Feelings that are counterproductive when you choose to coparent with someone.
5. Coparenting can become messy when coparents continue to be intimate after the relationship is over.
6. If you don't want to be with her don't hit it!
7. Find someone else to be intimate with and focus on raising the children together.

Guiding Questions:

1. Are there commitments I need to make in regard to this chapter?
2. If I am still intimate with my coparent, what are three things I can do to stop being intimate with her?
3. What opportunities for growth (if any) do I have in this area?

Challenge:

I challenge you to stop being intimate with your coparent if you haven't already. Depending on the situation this could be extremely difficult. Odds are there's a level of comfort and familiarity involved. If you're not going to be together you should stop. It may seem harmless, and you both may think it's ok. The reality is it complicates the situation. Boundaries need to be set and you need time and space to heal from each other. You both need closure and it's easier to coparent when you're not being intimate. Focus on coparenting and find someone else to be intimate with. Will you accept this challenge?

CHAPTER 7

Humbling Yourself

Pride cometh before the fall and pride is bound in the heart of a fool. The Bible has some jewels in it. It can be hard to admit when you are wrong or to see how you are wrong in a situation. We want to be right, and we want to win. So much so that we will argue a point knowing that we are wrong. Sometimes we have to eat a slice of humble pie. It is okay to admit that you were wrong about something and to apologize. It takes a big person to do this. Deny the urge to "win". What exactly are you winning? Sometimes you can win a battle and lose the war. Not that we are at war, but hopefully you get what I mean. Example, you get into an argument with your child's mother about money. She asks you for fifty dollars to buy uniform pants for your child. You feel like you have given enough and refuse to give her the money. It becomes an argument, and you begin taking shots at each other. You start saying the most hurtful things you can think of and belittling each other. You bring up a mistake from her past or an insecurity she has, to finish her off and shut her up. It works! You make her cry, and she gets off the phone. You win! You shut her up and she leaves you alone. A couple days go by, and you have not heard from her. You call and get no answer. A few more days go by and still no answer. It is time for your visit and she still does not answer. You miss time with your child. Now you are pissed and your child is upset because they wanted to see you. It's petty as hell, do you see what happened? You hurt her and she used the only thing she could to hurt you back. Your child. And guess who suffered? Your child.

These types of things happen every day. We swell up with pride and have emotional reactions with the women in our lives. We have to learn to control our emotions. We have to humble ourselves and not always be prideful. There is a time and place for everything. Sometimes we do have to stand our ground and hold firm to what we said or what we believe. Other times it is okay to let her win if it is a petty insignificant battle. This is situational and you will have to make a decision about when to stand your ground and when to let her win. Even if you do not let her win, there is a way to be humble and still get your point across. Not to mention you do not have to react to everything she does. Every action is not worthy of a reaction. Sometimes you have to hold your peace, shake your head and keep it moving. Choose your battles wisely. Some battles are not worth fighting. It is hard to tell someone they are right, especially when we are wrong, but it gets easier with time. Jay Z once said, "moral victories are for minor league coaches". I felt that in my soul. Stop trying to win petty battles and disputes and focus on the big picture. The big picture is your child being safe and healthy in a loving environment. It is your child being taken care of and growing up in a better situation than you did. At least that is my take on it.

Get out yo feelings! - Sometimes I get in my feelings and feel like I should not have to watch the children or I get mad because I had to watch them longer than I expected to. That is foolishness and I have to sit back and laugh at myself sometimes. Pride is what that is and pride is bound in the heart of a fool.

The reality is we should cherish the time we have with our children because as they get older and start to have their own lives we will see less and less of them. Enjoy your time with your children while you can. It can be challenging to balance your responsibilities, work or business, personal life and spending time with your children, but it must be done. We have to show up for our children. Get out "yo feelings" and enjoy your time with your children. I know you are probably busy and your plate may be full, but we must spend quality time with our children. They need it. It has been said that there is a blessing only a father can give. Our approval, acceptance, and support mean more than we will ever know. I have also heard people say a girl's father is her first love and her first heartbreak. When we look at the type of man we want our sons to be, we can see how much our presence is needed. In some instances, we need to show our sons how not to move, and how we turned our lives around after making mistakes that we do not want to see them make. Humble yourself or be humbled.

Chapter 7: Key Points, Guiding Questions & Challenges

Key Points In This Chapter:

1. It can be hard to admit when you are wrong or to see how you are wrong.
2. It is okay to admit that you were wrong about something and to apologize.
3. Some women will weaponize your children to get even with you.
4. If a woman weaponizes your child, you and your child miss opportunities to spend time together. Being humble is not a solution to this problem, but it can help to decrease instances of the woman feeling the need to weaponize your child.
5. Stop trying to win petty battles and disputes and focus on the big picture. The big picture is your child being safe and healthy in a loving environment. It is your child being taken care of and growing up in a better situation than you did.
6. Get out of your feelings about watching your children. Reframe your perspective to, " I get to spend time with my child" and then make the most of the time you have with them.
7. There is a blessing only a father can give his children.

Guiding Questions:

1. What commitments do I need to make in regard to this chapter?
2. Do I know how to humble myself? And how to stand firm when I need to?
3. What opportunities for growth do I have in this area?

Challenge:

I challenge you to humble yourself and begin doing the work to get your ego in check. We should take pride in who we are and have self-respect. However, we cannot afford to be prideful fools. You can work on this by thinking before you speak, taking a deep breath before you respond, reframing what you need to say, and becoming spiritually grounded. These are simply suggestions. You have to figure out what is going to help you humble yourself. There is a saying, "humble yourself or be humbled". It is important that we get this right.

CHAPTER 8

Healthy Boundaries

There have been seasons in which any and all communication was about my son. There have been times in which I felt this was the best and only way to operate. I did not want it to be this way, but it can reach a point where that's just what it is. Things can get so ugly that you may not need to be around your coparent or even talk to them. This is particularly rough with smaller children. We never want to be in this place, but it happens. If we reach this place maybe the only communication is about the child and the child's needs. Maybe you stay away from each other and arrange a pickup and drop off spot. No matter how ugly it gets, never stop being present for your children.

After a while it is wise to reconcile. You have to deal with your coparent one way or another. Ideally someone shows the maturity to work through the disagreement. When the olive branch is extended, be wise enough to accept it. You may have to be the one to extend it. Remember, the priority is the child. Do not be so full of foolish pride that you can not move past the offense and find a way back towards coparenting effectively. There are times when you have to set boundaries, enforce boundaries, and hold people accountable. Again, the thought process should be, am I doing what is best for my child? You can make the argument that your child needs to see you stand your ground and not tolerate disrespect. You may be correct in your argument. The bigger question is how does this impact your relationship with your child? Is there a visitation order in place? Are you missing time with your child over something silly? You shouldn't, but petty is glorified these days and some women weaponize children. Set your boundaries and use wisdom while doing so. As a man you should have non negotiables and standards that you stand on. I truly believe that. At the same time, you do not have to engage in every battle. There is a time and place for everything. It is important that you set boundaries and let people know where you stand. It may be uncomfortable for you based on your level of comfort with confrontation, however you will save yourself headaches by setting boundaries early and letting people know where you stand.

Respect the one you're with- Be mindful that your actions do not disrespect your current significant other. Not to say she will not feel disrespected by your actions, but be mindful of it and do your best to make sure she does not feel disrespected. That is complex so let's break it down. It is possible for you to do something and it be taken out of context. It is also possible that the woman you are with has an insecurity about your child's mother, her position in your life or something about herself. Since these are possibilities, you have to be mindful of how you move. Your wife or the woman you are currently dating should be your priority and you can not allow your coparent to run your house and or your life. Otherwise go be with her and do not waste another woman's time. You have to be able to decipher between "I might be doing too much", and "she trippin". It's a thin line, a really thin line. For example, you are having an important conversation about your child on the phone and your woman wants you off that phone now! She can clearly see your conversation is about your child and you are assisting with a challenging matter. She trippin! Or she is upset because her friend video calls her and shows her the three of you in the mall laughing, joking and shopping. You did not tell her where you were going and have not spoken to her. She calls you to see what is going on and you ignore her call. When approached about the situation you get defensive and flip out on her. You trippin! You didn't communicate or ask how she felt about you going to the mall, you didn't empathize or acknowledge her feelings, you did not answer her phone call, and you became defensive and flipped on her when you were wrong. You could have given your child's mother money to go shopping or went shopping with your woman and your child. I could make up other scenarios, but you get the point. Be mindful of how you move and do your best not to disrespect your woman.

If for some reason your significant other does feel disrespected. Have a conversation with her. Do not become defensive as I have in the past. Listen to what she is saying. Then ask yourself if you would feel disrespected if the roles were reversed. Even if you would not, honor her feelings and think through what you can do differently to avoid her feeling this way in the future. This is not easy, but neither is coparenting. For example, your woman tells you she feels like you spend too much time talking to your coparent. This is a moment for self-inspection. Are you talking to her too much? That is, are you giving her more attention than your woman? Are you giving your coparent time and attention your woman feels like should be hers? If so, she may have a valid complaint. Realistically you have to talk to your coparent in order to coparent effectively. The conversation should largely be about your child. You may discuss other topics. You may advise her, encourage her, uplift her or so on and so forth. Are you giving your woman that same energy? If you are not giving her that same energy and more then it is a problem. You are with your new woman and she should be the priority. You can't be tripping on what's behind you. Otherwise, you run the risk of losing the woman you are with. There's a line! Be present for your coparent, but take care of your lady first. Shout out to my wife for being by my side and helping me with my son. She picks him up from school, cooks for him, retwists his locs, loves him and treats him like her own. That's a life hack. Having a loving, caring, nurturing wife is clutch. I am a great father, but my partner in crime, she is the real MVP.

Respect your coparent publicly and privately especially in front of the kids- I want to say your child's mother is a reflection of you. However, that would be extreme and may not necessarily be true. What is true is that you should not disrespect her publicly or in private. It's not a good look. It's easy to get caught up in an emotional battle with a woman, however when we do this we lose. Take the high road and do not be messy. At the end of the day, she was good enough to lay down with, sleep with, or whatever you two did. So you should not be dogging her on social media, making posts about her or badmouthing her to other people. It will not change the situation or make it better. Do not be petty or put everyone in your business. Everything ain't for everybody. Set the boundary with yourself that you will not bash her on social media, expose her, or go back and forth with her. I mean think about how that sounds, I'm exposing my child's mother? I know, it can be challenging, you want to tell your side of the story, you wanna be petty cause she's petty, I get it. It is not a good look bro. LIG it (let it go). Take the high road.

Chapter 8: Key Points, Guiding Questions & Challenges

Key Points From This Chapter:

1. No matter how ugly it gets, never stop being present for your children.
2. There are times when you have to set boundaries, enforce boundaries, and hold people accountable.
3. Set your boundaries and use wisdom while doing so.
4. Respect your coparent publicly and privately.
5. As a man, you should have non negotiables and standards that you stand on. At the same time you do not have to fight every battle.
6. Be mindful that your actions do not disrespect your current significant other.
7. Your wife or the woman you're currently dating should be your priority and you cannot allow your coparent to run your house and or life.
8. Be present for your coparent but take care of your lady first.
9. Set the boundary with yourself that you will not bash your coparent on social media, expose her, or go back and forth with her.

Guiding Questions:

1. Do I have healthy boundaries in place?
2. What boundaries do I need to set with my coparent?
3. What opportunities for growth do I have in this area?

Challenge:

I challenge you to reassess the boundaries you have in place with your coparent. Are the boundaries you currently have in place sufficient? You set boundaries, enforce boundaries, and hold people accountable. I can not tell you what this looks like in your given situation, but if the woman you are currently with feels disrespected by the way you engage with your coparent, you may need to take a look at that and potentially make some adjustments.

CHAPTER 9

Postpartum Depression

According to the Merriam-Webster Dictionary, postpartum depression is a mood disorder involving intense psychological depression that typically occurs within one month after giving birth, lasts more than two weeks, and is accompanied by other symptoms (such as social withdrawal, difficulty in bonding with the baby, and feelings of worthlessness or guilt)

I am not qualified to speak on postpartum depression from a medical standpoint. I have a limited understanding of it and I was not the most supportive when my son's mother went through it. Actually, that qualifies me to tell you how not to handle it. What I can tell you is that it is real. Women go through it and it is a really difficult time for them. What we cannot do is be dismissive. We cannot turn a blind eye to what our coparent is saying and feeling. If postpartum depression comes up, we need to be attentive, supportive, and on point. Even if we do not know what to do, we can find someone who does, or look up resources to help her out. Like I said I do not completely understand it, but I do know women go through it. I dropped the ball when my son's mother told me about it, and I have seen other men drop the ball which is why I felt the need to address it. I have seen the resentment that can arise when we get this wrong and it can be avoided by us taking the situation seriously and doing what we can to help our coparent through it. If you don't know what to do, look up resources online, speak to other women you know about it, listen to what she has to say, and whatever you do do not write it off. We do not get to make that call. Avoid the resentment and get it right. Listen, take postpartum depression seriously, and be supportive.

I could not wrap my mind around the idea at first mainly because my mother was superwoman in many ways. I felt like she was being weak and making the whole thing up to get out of being a mom. I was wrong for that and it was a lesson I had to learn the hard way. By the grace of God nothing crazy happened as a result of my dismissiveness. Dismissing postpartum can end up going terribly wrong for the mother and the child. We have to take postpartum depression seriously and support the mother of our children if she is experiencing it. Even if she doesn't flat out say "I have postpartum depression", keep an eye on her after she gives birth to your child. Watch out for signs and symptoms of depression and any behaviors she exhibits outside of her norm. Check in regularly and ask her how she's feeling. Again, we have to take this seriously and be supportive.

Resource list:

The National Maternal Mental Health Hotline- 1-833-9-HELPMOMS (1-800-943-5746) https://postpartumstress.com

www.betterhelp.com

Chapter 9: Key Points, Guiding Questions & Challenges

Key points from this chapter:
1. Postpartum depression is real. We need to take it seriously if it comes up and be supportive to the women in our lives.
2. We do not have to be experts on the topic, but we should keep an eye on the mother of our child after childbirth and consult a medical professional if needed. We can also talk to women in our lives that we know and trust or research the topic to better understand how we can be supportive.

Guiding Question
1. What commitment do I need to make in regards to this Chapter? (If Any)

Your coparent may or may not have experienced postpartum depression. Either way we have to raise awareness around postpartum.

Challenge:
I challenge you to help raise awareness around postpartum depression. Have a conversation with a woman you know and trust about it, research it, or speak with a medical professional. After you complete that, share what you learn with a man in your life. We can collectively gain a better understanding of postpartum and be more supportive of the women in our lives if and when they experience it.

CHAPTER 10

Gift Giving

One thing I have always done was buy gifts for my coparent from my son. I know she likes it and in turn she reciprocates it. As my son has gotten older, he actually goes into stores and picks gifts out himself. Sometimes he pays for the gifts with his own money. Even if he cannot make it to the store or forgets, I get her a gift from him. Yes, even when I am not feeling her, I still do. I know she appreciates it. To take it a step further I believe gift giving may be her love language. Not simply because she likes gifts, but because of how she reacts when she gets gifts. Also because of the way she buys my son's gifts. You see a lot when you pay attention. By no means is this a requirement or something you need to do. You may be saying to yourself, "This dude doing too much" What I can say is this works for me. Society can make you feel like you are worthless if you do not have a valentine or get a present for your birthday. I do not agree with this method of thinking, but I acknowledge that many people do. If taking your child to buy their mom a present is going to make her feel special and give you points, why not do it? Small inconvenience for a potentially large reward. This may look like buying roses or flowers for Mother's Day, or her birthday. It could be the child making a Valentine's Day card and giving her a piece of candy or helping your child make her a gift for Christmas. This is also a way to teach your child the importance of giving and gift giving. If your child's mother is unappreciative or unreceptive to gift giving, then fall back. It is worth a shot though.

Chapter 10: Key Points, Guiding Questions & Challenges

Key points from this chapter:

1. Gift giving can be a beautiful thing under certain circumstances.
2. Your coparent has to be in a place to receive the gift.
3. The gift is from your child and not from you.
4. You can buy a gift or help your child make a gift.
5. Use good judgment when buying gifts.
6. If your coparent is not in a place to receive gifts or unappreciative, forget I ever said this.

Guiding Questions:

1. Are you open to helping your child make or purchase a gift for their mother?
2. Do I already do this? If so, what are some gifts my child's mother would appreciate from my child? (You can refer back to this list during the holidays)
3. What opportunities for growth do I have in this area?

Challenge:

I challenge you to help your child create or purchase a gift for your coparent. You could help them make a thank you card, an arts and crafts project, or take them to purchase a gift. It's a nice gesture and It's worth a shot. If it goes well, consider making it a practice. If it doesn't, no harm, no foul.

CHAPTER 11

Forgiveness

Forgive yourself for the relationship not working out. She may blame you for the failed relationship, remind you of how you hurt her or how you did not support her or provide for her. Forgive yourself and move forward. Ideally, you are not the same man you were then (hopefully). You have grown, invested in yourself, matured, and you are in a different place. You can't change what you've done, but you can change how you do things.

Focus on your relationship with your children. Their opinion is the only one that matters. You need to be present for them and actively involved in their life. Some people will hold the mistakes of your past over your head forever if you allow them to. You did what you did or didn't do what you didn't do. You don't have to keep beating yourself up for it or allow anyone else to. You do not have to walk around feeling guilty because the relationship did not work out. It happens. Forgive yourself, be the best dad you can be and move forward with your life. Give yourself permission to be forgiven. If you don't feel like you can, then I give you permission to be forgiven. You are not your past and you are not your mistakes. Her opinion of you is none of your business. You cannot keep beating yourself up or allowing her to beat you up over mistakes you made in the past. Operate in the present.

You may need to forgive yourself for not being present for your children. Yes we should be present for our children, yes we should provide for them, protect them, teach them and make them feel loved. However, if you did not do all of those things, I encourage you to start. You cannot go back in time and do things differently. Every day is a new opportunity, a new chance to get it right. You may have messed up. If you have an opportunity to start developing a relationship with your child, then do it! Forgive yourself for not being present, apologize to your child, and begin the healing process. You cannot control how your child responds to you. My mom always said nothing beats a failure, but a try. You owe it to your children and to yourself to try to make it right. There are no guarantees but go for it! There's no perfect parent. Forgive yourself and do everything you can to make it right with your child. It may be necessary to consult a family counselor to help you work through your issues. You may need to see a counselor for yourself. Whatever work needs to be done, man up and do it.

Some children and adults are manipulative and will hold the mistakes you made over your head. This is another reason why I say forgive yourself. You cannot allow your children to punish you over and over for your shortcomings. You may have got it wrong, but you should not have to pay for your mistakes every time someone gets upset. Learn to forgive yourself.

Forgive her-Forgive her for whatever she did or didn't do. Not for her, but for yourself. It takes too much energy to walk around mad at someone. You cannot afford to walk around angry and getting upset every time you see her. You are robbing yourself of joy and children pick up on things like that. Forgive and move on. Even if things are not honky dory and you are not coparenting on a high level. Be cordial. Your children should see you be respectful to their mother. They do not need to see you two disrespect each other, avoid each other or not be on speaking terms. Again, every situation is unique and there may be legal orders in place. I am not suggesting that you violate an order that has been put in place. I am saying if there is no order in place for you two, at least be cordial. It has been said that not forgiving someone is like drinking poison waiting for them to die. That always resonated with me. Forgive and move forward. You are not your mistakes or your shortcomings as a man. You're human, and as humans we are all imperfect and have made mistakes. Do not allow people to punish you over and over for your mistakes. Forgive, live, and let live.

Chapter 11: Key Points, Guiding Questions & Challenges

Key Points In This Chapter:

1. Forgive yourself and move forward.
2. Your child's opinion of you is the only one you should be concerned with.
3. Do not allow people to hold the mistakes of your past over your head.
4. Be the best dad you can be and move forward with your life.
5. You cannot go back in time and do things differently. Every day is a new opportunity, a new chance to get it right.
6. You cannot allow your children to punish you over and over for your shortcomings. You may have got it wrong, but you should not have to pay for your mistakes every time someone gets upset.
7. Forgive Her. Not for her, but for yourself. It takes too much energy to walk around mad at someone.

Guiding Questions:

1. What do I need to forgive myself for?
2. What do I need to forgive my son's mother for?
3. What opportunities for growth do I have in this area?

Challenge:

I challenge you to forgive yourself if you have not already. Forgive yourself for whatever you have done or have not done. Stop allowing people to weaponize your mistakes and shortcomings. Stop carrying that guilt and beating yourself up. Forgive yourself, pick your head up and make every effort you can to be involved in your child's life. Depending on your situation it could be a process, but it's worth it. I promise. You are forgiven! Now forgive yourself and move forward.

Bonus Challenges

Challenge 1.

I challenge you to be nicer to your coparent. I'm tryna help you out bro. Maybe you get results from your child's mother by giving her the silent treatment, being mean, aggressive, or hostile. If so, by all means do your thing. If you're not getting the results you would like, I encourage you to try a different approach. At least try. She might say you are only being nice because you want something, and although that's true, do it anyway. What you want is a better relationship with her which will ultimately benefit your child. Keep your mind on the mission. Get past the petty foolishness and drama that does not serve you so that you can work towards having a positive relationship and coparent on the next level. "Ain't nothing sweet", but be nicer to her and see what kind of results you get. It is going to take time; you cannot be nice one day and then say it did not work. Again, we're developing new norms, and this takes time and patience, but it's worth it in the end.

Challenge 2:

I challenge you to become a bridge builder. Oftentimes there is a win win situation. We just haven't developed the mindset to see these situations. Partially because of the lens we look at situations with and partially because we want to win. You stand on one side of an issue or have your viewpoint on a situation and she may have a different opinion. When we learn to build bridges, we learn to look for the compromise in a situation. There may not always be a compromise you can make without compromising your terms as a man. However, we should be asking ourselves, how can I build a bridge and we meet in the middle?

Challenge 3:

I challenge you to accept your child's mother for who she is. My mother always said "a leopard don't change its stripes". There is some truth to that statement. Sometimes what we see is what we get. I am not saying accept her for who she is and be with her. I am saying accept her for who she is because she may not change her ways and think through what you need to do to coparent with her. I do not know the mother of your child and every person is different. For some this could mean accepting that she has a smart mouth and sticking to the facts when you communicate with her so that you don't get upset or get into an argument. Or understanding that she is late everywhere she goes and giving a cushion time for events or picking your child up yourself instead of waiting on her to drop the child off. For others your child's mother could be extremely toxic and have unresolved issues that she needs to deal with. She might have high energy and be a lot to take in. Again, accept her for who she is and think through what you can do to coparent with her more effectively. You cannot change other people. People have to want to change and change themselves. So why spend time being frustrated about how your child's mother behaves. You can encourage her to make changes, better herself, or seek counseling, but you cannot change her. Only she can do that. Sometimes we have to accept people for who they are and deal with them accordingly.

Conclusion

I want to start by thanking you for reading this book. Coparenting is something we do not discuss enough and that needs to be addressed. If we can take the time to intentionally focus on becoming better coparents, I believe our children will be all the better for it. If we can work together to do what is in the best interest of our children, I believe we will see better results through our children. The reality is that we can. It's possible for us to be cordial to our coparent, work together with our coparent, and even become friends with our coparent. Both parents will have to step out of their comfort zone in order to improve the relationship. It is going to require work from both parties and it probably will not be easy, but it will be worth it. The effort I have put into my relationship with my coparent is a gift that keeps on giving. We still disagree at times and have an occasional flare up, but I would take that over the place we were in 10 years ago any day of the week. There was constant bickering and arguing, pissing matches, ego driven arguments, petty matches, disrespect, toxic behavior, legal proceedings, and at some points hatred for each other. We have come so far from that place that you would not believe how bad it was if you sat in a room with us. I am proud of us and the work we have put in to reach a place where our focus is working together to do what is best for our child. I share that to say if we can do it, some of you can too. For some, pride will get in the way and that's sad. It's sad because some people would rather be right than to do what's right for their children. Some people are so hurt, so angry, so disappointed, that they cannot get past the failed relationship to get to a place where they can work together to do what is best for their children. Please don't let that be you. I sincerely pray and hope that all coparents can work through their issues and coparent on a higher level. Call me a dreamer. As men we should hold a strong context and show up powerfully. I am not saying women should have a pass to act out or demonstrate toxic behavior. I am saying we should be steadfast and unmovable when it comes to our children. There is no compromising with some people and some people will not change no matter what you do. I think back to a heated discussion with my son's mother, ok it was an argument. And during that argument I remember saying I'm not going to leave my son how your father left you! And there was silence for a moment. Some women have daddy issues and unresolved issues they need to deal with. For some women all they have ever experienced is men disappointing them and leaving them. It is possible that a woman may see you as another man who left her. Some women have never truly been around a man and they do not understand men. All they know about men is what they see on tv or what they grew up hearing their aunts and mom say about men. This is not your problem and I am not saying you should try to change their perception. As men we should not have to pay for the mistakes of the men that came before us. I'm saying that because this is the case with many women we should show them that we are going to be there for our children no matter what. That no matter what they do we choose to be fathers and be involved in our children's lives. I know, it's not fair. We should not have to jump through leaps and bounds to be involved in our children's lives. We should not have to deal with the drama and the toxic behavior. Hell hath no fury like a woman's scorn and sometimes we play a part in the way they act or engage with us. Whether it be that we sold them a dream, left them for another woman or just flat out told them we didn't want them anymore. The reason is not important. The point is sometimes we play a part in the way our coparents engage with us. I'm not saying who's right and who's wrong. I'm saying we need to take ownership for what we did or didn't do and sometimes we need to sincerely apologize in order to begin the path forward. Ultimately you will not have to answer to your coparent. Relationships end and people move on. You will have to answer to your child. Your child will want to know why you were not there for them. You can blame their mother. The question I beg you to ask yourself is "have I done everything in my power to have a relationship with my child?" Well have you? If you haven't, what do you need to do? If you can truly say you have done everything in your power to have a relationship with your child and be actively involved in their life then hats off to you. If you can't then it's time to get to work. Women should not raise our children alone. Children benefit from having their mother and father actively involved in their lives. Assuming there aren't any underlying issues, neglect or abuse involved. Some people are not fit to raise children. Assuming you are, you should be involved in your child's life. If you are not in a place to be able to raise your child, I encourage you to sign up for parenting classes and take steps towards being in a place to be able to have a relationship with your child.

I have expressed how important coparenting is and shared some of the things that have worked for me. I hope that something I said resonates with you and helps you to coparent more effectively. Ain't nothin to it but to do it! The ball is in your court now. Do what you need to do to coparent on a higher level and be actively involved in your child's life. I love you and your children and I wish you nothing but the best.

Notes

Notes

Notes

Notes

Follow Us on Social Media

Let's Get Connected for Our Latest Content & Updates

- on IG @adverstybuildscharacter

- on TikTok @adversitybuildscharacter

- on YouTube @adversitybuildscharacter7768

Made in United States
Orlando, FL
29 April 2024